Chapter One

Santa yawned and also stretched. He opened initially one eye and afterwards the other. He smiled at Mrs Claus, that was standing in front of him, with a mug of hot tea in one hand as well as a plate of her special delicious chocolate chip cookies in the other.

" Good morning, Santy!" she claimed, with a cozy smile as well as a twinkle in her eye. "Here's your tea, just the way you like it. One sugar dice and a little milk. As well as your preferred chocolate chip cookies!"

" Ah, thanks, Mrs Claus!" said Santa. He took a sip of the tea as well as a huge bite of a cookie.

" Are you thrilled concerning today?" asked Mrs Claus. "I most absolutely am!" said Santa.

Santa had actually spent most of the year eating and also oversleeping front of the crackling fire. However his time of remainder was over. He would be extremely busy for the following twenty 4 days. When he was going to make a browse through to his reindeer and also elves, as well as today was the day. He hadn't seen them in a long while and also he made certain they would all be getting excited concerning the big trip on Christmas Eve.

There is so much to do! assumed Santa. After I complete my tea as well as cookies, I'll head out to the stables to look at the reindeer. Then, I'll see exactly how the fairies are carrying out in the workshop.

" I've been reading several of the letters we've obtained from youngsters all over the globe," claimed Mrs Claus. "Listen to this set. It's from a young boy called Blaine. He's 6 years old as well as he stays in the United States, from Ohio."

" Oh, take place!" stated Santa, choosing some cookie crumbs out of his lengthy, white beard. "I enjoy checking out these letters!"

Mrs Claus pressed her analysis glasses up her nose as well as began checking out. Dear Santa Claus,

Exactly how are you? I wish that it's not also cold at the North Pole.

I have actually been actually, actually great this year. When my mama tells me

to, I take my pet for a stroll every day as well as I constantly cleanse my area.
Well, a lot of the time.

Santa, I truly want a remote regulated auto for Christmas. I do not desire any
clothes though.

Love Blaine

" Oh, I like that a person!" said Santa. His bright, blue eyes shimmered under
his bushy white eyebrows. "Read me another one, Mrs Claus!"

Mrs Claus drew another letter from a huge sack as well as started to check
out. Beloved Santa,

Just how are your reindeer? Did they like the carrots that I left for them last
year? Santa, in 2015 I asked for more lego however you offered me an infant
sister instead. Could I please have some lego this year?

Love Josh

P.S. I will certainly leave you a glass of milk as well as you can consume several
of the gingerbread house that my mother makes every year. I will additionally
leave even more carrots for your reindeer.

" Ho, Ho, Ho!" claimed Santa. He chuckled so difficult his huge stubborn belly
wobbled. "We'll need to make sure Josh obtains his lego!"

As the fire snapped in the cozy log home, Santa as well as Mrs Claus read
some even more letters. He stood up and also provided another huge stretch
when Santa had actually finished all of his cookies. He was eagerly anticipating
getting going on all the work that needed to be done. He wanted to see to it
that every young boy and lady obtained a special present.

" Are you going to get started, Santy?" asked Mrs Claus.

" I certain am," stated Santa. "The initial point I'm going to do is look at the
reindeer!"

" Oh yes!" said Mrs Claus. "I saw Donner, Blitzen and also Cupid in the lawn
the other day! I told them to anticipate a browse through from you any day!"

" Well, I'm mosting likely to look at them currently, Mrs Claus," stated Santa.
"I'll be back in a while."

" I'll have a wonderful, big pot of stew waiting on you when you get back," claimed Mrs Claus. "Then we can read more letters!"

" That sounds good!" claimed Santa. "I'll see you later."

Santa put on his huge jacket and also his knee high, black boots that Mrs Claus had put out for him. He pulled a woollen, green hat down over his ears and covered a long, red headscarf around his neck. Last but not least, he placed on his thick handwear covers.

With a chuckle and also a wave goodbye to Mrs Claus, he opened the door and also headed to the huge stables in the distance. He could not wait to see the reindeer.

Chapter Two

As Santa Claus walked to the stables, he looked up at the grey sky. It would not be light for a lot longer. In winter season, the daytime just lasted for a short time. Santa enjoyed this time of year.

He unlocked to the steady and tipped within. To his left was a huge location where the sleigh was. The sleigh that would certainly take a trip high in the evening sky, throughout the globe, on Christmas Eve.

It was when he took a closer check out the sleigh that his pleased smile turned into a frown. The usual glossy sleigh wasn't shiny anymore. Santa went back in surprise. The red paint was worn and damaged. The gold trim was plain.

Frowning, he looked inside the huge sleigh. He gasped. The red velvet seats were torn as well as ripped. He after that heard some rustling. Overlooking, he could not think what he saw. Mice! Some were sleeping, snuggled together, and others were scooting to and fro.

I can't think this! assumed Santa. What in tarnation is going on? Simply wait until I speak with Norman!

Norman was one of Santa's fairies. When it wasn't being utilized, he was in charge of the reindeer and also of maintaining the sleigh glossy and also tidy. Norman had constantly done a great work. What had occurred this year?

I'm certain there's a good factor for this, thought Santa. I'll speak to Norman and he'll need to obtain the sleigh figured out. It's not a big bargain.

Santa then strolled farther down into the stables. He could see two reindeer resting in some hay. A delighted smile moved his mouth.

" Hey Dancer, hi Prancer!" claimed Santa, now smiling happily. "Hello, Boss!"

claimed Dancer and Prancer. "It's great to see you!"

" It's remarkable to see you too, my friends!" said Santa. "Only twenty 4 days to go up until our big trip! Are you as thrilled as I am?"

" , I'm not sure," stated Dancer. He traded a worried look with Prancer.

"Whatever is the matter?" asked Santa.

Without stating a word, both of the reindeer rose as well as began strolling in the direction of Santa. Santa's jaw dropped. Dancer and Prancer were both strolling with a limp. A bad limp.

" What took place to you both?" asked Santa, taking a look at them in shock.

Prancer as well as Dancer considered each various other again. They both hung their heads.

" You tell him," claimed Dancer. "No, you inform him," said Prancer.

" Tell me what?" asked Santa, really feeling very stressed. Dancer spoke.

" Two nights back, Prancer and I went to a barn dancing," he said. "It wasn't too away, so we believed why not go. You recognize barn dancings are normally a hoot."

" But, well, we type of got lugged away," claimed Prancer. "What do you indicate?" asked Santa, really feeling baffled.

" Everyone was having fun at the barn dance," stated Dancer. "Then, Prancer and I believed it would certainly be enjoyable to dance on the table."

" The only thing is," stated Prancer, "it ended up being not such an excellent concept. We, uh, we diminished the table!"

" You diminished the table?" exclaimed Santa.

" Yup," claimed Dancer, with a sigh. "I sprained my ankle."

" And I pulled a muscle mass," said Prancer, looking embarrassed. "I can hardly walk."

Santa was so stunned he didn't know what to state. He just looked at them. How could this have taken place? They had the big trip to go on! Exactly how were Dancer and also Prancer mosting likely to make it?

" I'm so sorry, Boss!" said Dancer. "We feel like morons!"

" And I hate to inform you, yet there's some other bad news!" claimed Prancer.

" What else could perhaps be wrong?" cried Santa. He wrung his hands with each other and nervously tugged at his lengthy mustache.

" Walter is gone," claimed Dancer.

" Walter's gone? Where?" asked Santa. Walter was a wonderful reindeer. What did they mean he was gone?

" He moved!" stated Prancer. "I know it's unsubstantiated, but he migrated! We tried to chat him out of it however he would not pay attention!"

Santa wheezed. It was true that reindeer moved. Prior to winter months, they would normally head southern, to discover locations that weren't as cool as the North Pole. Santa's reindeer really did not migrate. They stuck with Santa all year round. They didn't wish to move. Life was also good at Santa's place. This had never ever occurred before!

" Walter just felt the call of the wild!" stated Dancer. "He ran into a few of his old pals and that was it. He went off with them."

" Oh deer, oh deer!" sobbed Santa. "I can't think what you're informing me!"

Professional dancer and also Prancer took a look at each various other. Just how could they tell Santa that there was much more trouble? They understood they had to. So, they informed Santa that there was an additional piece of trouble.

" What else could perhaps have taken place?" asked Santa, in misery. He was nearly all set to weep.

Dancer and Prancer really did not address him. Instead, Dancer discharged a whistle and also proclaimed, "SPRINGER! COME HERE!"

They all looked as Springer came into view, strolling in the direction of them. She was strolling quite gradually. Santa allowed out the largest gasp he had let out that day when she obtained right into sight. He looked at Springer's big belly.

" I have information to tell you," stated Springer. "As you can see, I'm pregnant! My child schedules in January. I won't have the ability to assist draw the sleigh at Christmas. I'm so sorry!"

Santa drank his head in disbelief. This had never ever occurred prior to. Reindeer never had their children in winter season. "This is ... is ... highly uncommon," he finally sputtered.

" I understand, Boss, I know!" said Springer. "It's a wonder, a real wonder!"

" Yes, yes it is," claimed Santa. "Now, you just take excellent treatment of yourself, Springer." He looked to Dancer and Prancer. "Please inform me there's absolutely nothing else!"

" No Boss," they claimed. "Thankfully, not!"

Prancer after that gave one more loud piercing whistle. Soon, the other reindeer came trotting into the stable, their unguis clattering on the flooring. "The manager is below!" yelled Prancer. "Come greet!"

Santa was soothed to see that the various other reindeer were all great and also he gave them all a rub and a rub as they nuzzled approximately him.

However when he left the secure, he had an instead heavy heart. He simply might not believe it. The sleigh looked old and also shabby as well as he had four reindeer that would not have the ability to make the trip at Christmas. Whatever was he mosting likely to do? Reindeer currently of year were hard to locate around the North Pole.

Something would have to be done. He simply wasn't certain what. He advanced to the massive workshop where the elves were. The first thing he required to do was to find Norman, the elf in charge of the sleigh and reindeer. Norman would have a great deal of clarifying to do. It was his work to keep the sleigh in tip top form and also to take treatment of the reindeer. Points can not get any type of even worse, can they? assumed Santa. Well, that's what he thought

Chapter Three

When Santa unlocked to the fairies workshop, he checked out. He hadn't been in the workshop for a long period of time. Where he was standing, he might see all three floors.

He walked through the first stage, seeing the elves as they worked with the production line. There were elves on the remote control vehicle production line, seriously covering them in brilliantly tinted covering paper. He visited another production line where fairies were covering boxes of lego.

" Oh, I love lego! I'll need to make certain that Josh gets his lego!" claimed Santa, thinking about the child who had actually composed the letter.

As Santa carried on, he saw assembly lines for jewellry making sets, soccer rounds and also watches. He viewed as the fairies seriously wrapped them. Santa responded approvingly with a little smile. These were all points that kids had requested in their letters.

" Wonderful!" he stated. "Absolutely wonderful!"

As Santa relocated with the floorings, throughout the setting up lines, he realized that something was incorrect. It was noticeable what it was. Currently of year, the workshop was generally like a hectic beehive, with countless fairies busy at the workplace. They often sang as they placed and also wrapped name tags on the here and now.

Yet the workshop wasn't such as an active beehive at all! It was only about half complete. Where were all the fairies? Xmas Eve was only twenty four days away! Every fairy was required to wrap the presents. They would certainly never ever get made with half the fairies gone!

Santa walked to the very back of the workshop, where the elves need to have been loading presents right into substantial sacks. There was nobody there. Not also one fairy! Lots of gifts were piled up. Presents that need to have been currently loaded into sacks.

Santa let and frowned out a huff. He marched to an additional component of the workshop, where the family room was. This was the room the fairies mosted likely to for their breaks.

When Santa opened the door to the rec space, he was stunned! The rec area was full of fairies! As opposed to working in the workshop, they were done in the rec area. Some were consuming egg nog. Others were sound asleep, huddled on the sofas, snoring away.

Numerous were playing computer game, watching television or playing cards. The one thing they weren't doing was operating in the workshop, covering Christmas offers for kids and also women throughout the world!

Then Santa spotted Fergus. He was very easy to place. His ears were exceptionally lengthy as well as pointy. He additionally had brilliant red hair which stood out all over the place. Fergus was in charge of packing the presents into sacks. Santa stalked Fergus.

" Fergus!" he shouted, seeming very frustrated. "What's going on below?" When a lot of the elves heard Santa's voice, they nudged each other as well as sat up straighter. It was the very first time that Santa had been in the workshop that year. Fergus leapt when Santa's voice boomed in his ear.

" Oh, Boss! I didn't see you there!" claimed Fergus, looking way up at Santa.

" Well, you can see me currently!" huffed Santa. "Now, inform me. Why are you and also your elves not packing presents into sacks?"

" Oh, well, ... we're just having a break," claimed Fergus. His cheeks were turning as red as his hair as he talked.

" From the appearances of it, it's been a quite long break!" grew Santa. "Half the elves are missing on the assembly lines! And also Fergus, there's an area filled with presents waiting to be packed into sacks!"

Fergus hung his head. The whole area came to be silent. No one attempted say a word. When he was around his growing laugh can generally be heard all over the workshop, Santa was typically satisfied as well as playful as well as. But there were no laughs now.

" I can not believe what is happening right here!" grew Santa. "You've had most of the year off! You must all be hectic in the workshop!"

Nobody stated anything. Santa checked out the space. He really can not believe the view prior to his eyes. This was the first time, ever before, that anything such as this had ever before occurred.

" Where's Norman?" Santa instantly asked. Santa checked out for the elf who was in charge of the sleigh and reindeers. "I need to speak with Norman right now about the sleigh as well as reindeer!"

" Norman's not right here," stated Smithie, a young fairy that ought to have been on the assembly line wrapping story books.

" Well, where is he?" snapped Santa, getting more frustrated by the minute.

" He's ... um ... he's in Florida!" said Freckles, one more fairy whose face was covered with a splattering of blemishes.

" FLORIDA?" barked Santa. "What on earth is he carrying out in Florida?"

" He went there on vacation," shrugged Fergus. "He claimed he wished to stay there a bit longer since it's wonderful and warm."

" This is horrendous!" yelled Santa. "In twenty 4 days, we have Christmas gifts to supply to children all over the world! As well as yet you all appear to believe you're on some sort of vacation!"

" Calm down, Boss," stated Smithie. "We'll get all the gifts filled and also wrapped into the sacks! There's great deals of time!"

" NO!" rumbled Santa, his cheeks a rosy red. "There's not a lot of time! I've gone through the workshop. If we're going to be ready for Christmas, you all require to get splitting!"

" We'll do the job, Boss!" stated Fergus. "Just loosen up! Relax!"

" CHILL OUT? KICK BACK?" yelled Santa. He looked around, looking at everybody. "What is taking place right here? Does any person have anything else to state?"

No one claimed a word. The only audios that could be listened to were snores and also whistles. A lot of fairies were still resting as well as had not heard a word that Santa had said.

" Well, this does it!" stated Santa. As well as he turned around and also stomped out of the workshop.

He stomped all the way to his log home, huffing and puffing as he went. As he stomped along, he thought of what had actually occurred that day. Never ever in a million years might he have actually thought what was mosting likely to occur when he woke up that morning.

Exactly how are we mosting likely to prepare in twenty 4 days? thought Santa.
I don't have sufficient reindeer to draw the sleigh and there's no chance all
the presents are going to get covered in time. What am I going to do?
When he reached his log home, he unlocked and also pounded it shut behind
him. It was mosting likely to be a long evening. A very long night.

Chapter Four

When Santa strolled right into his log house, he removed his boots as well as dropped into his chair. He stared at the flames dance in the fireplace. Mrs Claus walked into the space.

" Santy!" she said loudly. "Why are you looking so glum? You were so excited when you left your house this morning!"

" Hmmph!" snorted Santa. "You are not going to think what happened this morning when I went to the workshop as well as the reindeer!"

Santa then informed Mrs Claus everything about his morning. Mrs Claus looked more and more shocked as Santa chatted. She gasped when Santa told her concerning Dancer and Prancer as well as their unsatisfactory legs. Her mouth dropped open when she listened to the news about Springer.

" Springer is going to have an infant?" she said loudly. "Why, that's never occurred prior to. Ever before!"

" I recognize!" said Santa. "And can you think that Walter migrated? Why would any reindeer intend to move when they have such an excellent life right here?"

She furrowed her brow when Santa informed Mrs Claus about the fairies.

"Hmmm," she said. "I'm stunned the fairies are acting by doing this! I question what's entered them?"

" I sure desire I knew," stated Santa. "I do not understand what's gotten involved in them. Normally they're busy as beavers and also happy to do their task."

" Oh, don't stress, Santy," claimed Mrs Claus, patting him on the shoulder. "We'll figure something out."

" But I don't recognize if we can!" exclaimed Santa. "The fairies are up until now behind wrapping presents that I do not recognize exactly how they'll ever before get captured up! And where are we mosting likely to discover four reindeer to change Dancer, Prancer and also Walter and Springer?"

" I don't recognize," stated Mrs Claus, "but we'll place our heads together and also see what we can think of. Now there's something I require you to do."

Mrs Claus then informed Santa that he needed to try on his red match. The special red suit that he would certainly be wearing for the huge journey. Santa hemmed and hawed. He actually had not been in the state of mind. However Mrs Claus told him he needed to attempt it on in case she needed to make changes.

With a grunt, Santa entered into his room. His red suit and also large, black belt were resting on the bed. He initially tried on the trousers. One pant leg as well as after that the other. There was a large issue, however. No matter just how difficult Santa tried, he can not get the trousers reconstructed around his stomach.

" How can this be?" he murmured, under his breath. He tried again to get his pants on, yet no matter just how much he twitched he could not obtain them around his stomach.

Santa tried on his red match. He already recognized, certainly, what would certainly take place. When he attempted to switch up the match, he could not reconstruct the switches. Not even shut.

" Mrs Claus!" yelled Santa. "Come here, fast!"

Mrs Claus came facing the room. She provided a grimace when she saw Santa. She had actually hesitated that this would happen.

" My match doesn't fit!" exclaimed Santa. "How can this be? I'm the very same size that I was last year!"

" I don't recognize how to tell you this Santy," stated Mrs Claus, "however you have actually been consuming a couple of even more pies recently!"

" Oh, bother!" said Santa. "Just what I need!"

"Don't stress, Santy," said Mrs Claus. "I'll just have to make you a new suit." She rapidly left the area to go locate the red velvet product that was saved in her wood trunk.

Santa went back to his huge, comfy chair by the fire. His face appeared like rumbling. He thought of the reindeer. He thought about the lazy fairies. He thought of his special suit being as well tight. Then, he thought of something that he can do to make himself really feel much better at that moment.

He went to his antique desk in the corner of the area as well as obtained an item of parched paper as well as a fountain pen. He began writing the advertisement that would go in papers around the elf world.

WANTED

Elves to operate in Santa Claus' workshop for following Christmas at the North Pole. Must be offered six weeks prior to Chirstmas Day. Need to want to strive!
Job summary- to cover Christmas offers for kids around the world. Uniform offered- red or green fit, sharp boots and jaunty hat.
Various other needs: must be under four feet tall, have a bright personality and also love to place a smile on youngsters's faces!
Santa sighed. He could not think what he was doing. He had actually never ever discharged anyone before in his life. He had never had to.
It was far too late to hire new fairies for this Christmas season. However following Christmas season, he would certainly have a brand-new group of elves!
He went back to his comfortable chair by the fire. Generally he would certainly fall asleep, but this time around, he could not. He believed and also thought and after that thought some more.
He thought again concerning the worn-out sleigh. He thought about the 4 reindeer that could not make the journey. He thought about all the lazy fairies that must have been hectic covering presents.
Mrs Claus came in with a dish of stew. Prior to she offered it to Santa, she reviewed the letter that he had left on his desk. Oh dear, she assumed. Santy is really distressed about all of this. Not that I condemn him!
" I see you're searching for brand-new staff, Santy," she claimed.
" Yes," stated Santa. "But I've been believing. I've got a new idea." "And what is that?" asked Mrs Claus.
" I've made a decision ..." Santa stopped. "I've decided ... I QUIT!" "WHAT?" said loudly Mrs Claus.
" Yes, you heard me ideal!" claimed Santa. "I've chosen I've had it! We're not mosting likely to do Christmas this year! Maybe not even following year! I quit!"
" But, Santy!" exclaimed Mrs Claus. "What about all the youngsters around

the globe that are anticipating a present from you? They'll be so let down!"
" Well, I'm not satisfied concerning that," grumbled Santa. "But I've made my choice. And also my choice is, I gave up!"
As well as with that said, he folded his arms as well as slumped back in his chair.

Chapter Five

For the next few days, Santa beinged in his comfortable chair brooding. He spent time staring into the fire while rubbing his large, orange cat that sat on his lap. Mrs Claus brought him mugs of hot tea. She really did not say excessive to him due to the fact that she understood he required time to himself. Rather, she worked on making his new suit.

It got on the 3rd day that the knock on the door came. Rap, rap, rap. 3 immediate knocks. Mrs Claus went to the door and also opened it.

" Fergus! Norman!" she exclaimed. Norman was the fairy accountable of the sleigh and also reindeer as well as Fergus was the elf in charge of filling today into the sacks.

" Hello, Mrs Claus," claimed Fergus. "We've come here to talk with Santa. We've got something really important to inform him."

" Come on in," claimed Mrs Claus, with a twinkle in her eye. "Santa is in his chair by the fire. Follow me."

Santa turned around when he heard all the footsteps going into the area. When he saw the 2 fairies with Mrs Claus, his jaw dropped in shock.

" Norman!" he said. "I thought you were in Florida!"

" Um, yeah, I was in Florida, yet I'm back now," claimed Norman, his ears and cheeks an intense red.

" How nice of you ahead back," stated Santa, giving him a gaze. "I thought you 'd stay in Florida longer to deal with your tan. And you, Fergus, I'm stunned you're not asleep on the sofa in the rec room."

There was a long pause. Norman as well as Fergus checked out each other. After that, they added to Santa as well as embraced him around his legs.

" Boss, I'm sorry!" claimed Norman. "I'm so sorry! I understand I ought to have been right here previously! I don't know what got into me!"

" And I'm sorry, as well!" stated Fergus. "Please forgive me, Boss!"

" I should claim," stated Santa, tugging at his beard. "I couldn't believe it when I heard that you were still in Florida, Norman. As well as what concerning the reindeer? I'm sure you've become aware of the problems we're having with them?"

" Listen Boss," said Norman. "I've been striving for the last two days on the reindeer issue. As well as I've resolved it!"

" You have?" stated Santa, in surprise.

" Yes!" said Norman, with a sorry search his face. "I've got 2 reindeer to replace Walter and also Springer!"

" Really?" exclaimed Santa, looking astonished. "How did you take care of to locate 2 reindeer on such brief notification?"

" I obtained fortunate," claimed Norman. "The various other day when I was tidying up the stables, Vixen can be found in. She was really delighted. She claimed there were two weird reindeer exterior."

" Well, that's extremely uncommon!" claimed Santa.

" It certain is! As a matter of fact, it's never happened before," stated Norman. "Anyways, I went sure as well as outdoors sufficient, there were 2 odd reindeer. It turns out they were lost."

" Lost?" said loudly Santa. "How did that occur?"

" They had actually moved down south a couple of months earlier," stated Norman. "But somehow, they got totally lost and also wound up walking around in circles. They wound up below, outside the stable! They've consented to stay and also assist draw the sleigh at Christmas, so currently we have adequate reindeer!"

" Amazing!" claimed Santa. "But what concerning Dancer as well as Prancer and also their lame legs?"

" That's taken care of as well," said Fergus. "I pled the doctor to find up as well as take a look at them. He claimed that if they rest from now till Christmas, they'll prepare just in time to go on the trip!"

" Well, I have to state that I'm pleased, Norman," claimed Santa. "Although I really hope this never ever occurs once more!"

" It won't, ever before," stated Norman. "And that's a promise!"

" This is all excellent and great," said Santa, "yet what regarding the fairies? They are method behind on wrapping the presents."

" We'll obtain the presents wrapped, Boss!" piped in Fergus. "I guarantee you, we'll get them done!" Fergus likewise looked extremely sorry. His lip shuddered and he appeared like he was going to cry.

Santa offered Fergus a hard appearance. "I've seen the workshop, Fergus. I truly don't know just how all the gifts can be wrapped in time!"

" We all had a large conference, everyone fairies," claimed Fergus. "We all know that we truly screwed up. A few of us were slouching." Fergus hung his head, looking embarrassed. "But we're all pulling together currently."

" You truly believe it can get done?" asked Santa doubtfully, rubbing his beard.

" We are going to work overtime," claimed Fergus. "Day and also night. I know we can do it. It's not far too late!"

" We'll get everything done," stated Norman. "And that's an assurance. We're mosting likely to make it approximately you, Boss!"

" Okay," claimed Santa, looking thoughtful. "I accept your apologies. As well as kids and women around the world are mosting likely to be as satisfied as can be!"

" Yes," claimed Fergus. "Most of all, we realized that we really did not intend to dissatisfy any kind of kids. We've obtained youngsters of our very own that are expecting presents from Santa, as well!"

Fergus as well as Norman after that entrusted to go back to the stables and the workshop. Santa settled back right into his comfortable chair as well as his orange pet cat jumped back onto his lap.

Mrs Claus came in with an additional mug of tea. "Here you go, Santy!" she stated. "I felt in one's bones that it would all exercise. I knew it!"

" I had not been so certain," said Santa, as he drank the hot tea. "But, I must claim, I'm extremely pleased with how everyone has gathered." "Only twenty even more days up until Christmas!" said Mrs Claus. "Yup," said Santa. "I can not wait!".
Mrs Claus breathed freely. She would never forget that most unusual day. The day Santa virtually quit.

Chapter Six

Finally, the big night had come. It was Christmas Eve. Mrs Claus laid Santa's new suit out on the bed. After Santa had trimmed his beard and mustache, he put the new suit on. When he walked out into the living room, Mrs Claus gasped.

"Santy, your new suit looks marvellous!" she said.

And it did. It fit Santa perfectly. The velvet material was bright red and the white trim was as white as could be. His new belt had a big, gold, shiny buckle and his new boots shone. His new hat fit perfectly on his head.

"Just one more thing," said Mrs Claus, and she handed Santa his gold rimmed glasses.

"Oh yes!" said Santa, "I don't want to forget these. I'm sure I'll have a lot of notes to read from children!"

Finally, under a midnight sky with bright, twinkling stars, Santa strode out to the stables with a lamp in his hand. Norman and his helpers were hitching the reindeer up to the sleigh. Santa let out a happy sound when he saw the sleigh.

"Why, it's beautiful!" he said. "It doesn't look like a wreck anymore!"

"It's been all cleaned and polished up," said Fergus. "It's a sight to behold once again!"

Santa then greeted the reindeer, giving them each a rub on the nose. "Dancer, Prancer, how are your legs?" he asked.

"I'm fine, Boss!" said Dancer. "My ankle healed just in time!"

"And I feel as good as new!" said Prancer. "The doc said we're well rested and good to go!"

"I hope you won't be dancing on tables anymore," said Santa. "At least, not anytime soon!"

"Oh no!" said Dancer. "And never again around Christmas!"

Santa was just about to ask where the two new reindeer were, when he heard the clicking sound of hooves on the wooden floor. Entering the stable were the two new reindeer, being led by one of the elves.

When they got to the sleigh, Norman introduced the new reindeer. "Santa, this is Comet," he said.

"Comet, so very pleased to meet you!" said Santa. "I can't tell you how lucky we are to have you!"

"And this here is Rudolph," said Norman, introducing the other reindeer.

Santa was shocked when he saw Rudolph, but he tried to hide it. The reason he was shocked was because of Rudolph's nose. His nose was big. Not just big, but a bright red. And not only was his nose big and bright red, but it glowed. In fact, it lit up the stables.

"So wonderful to meet you, Rudolph!" said Santa. "I tell you, it was meant to be that you and Comet got lost when you migrated! So happy to have both of you on our team!"

"Thank you so much, Santa!" said Rudolph, his face breaking into a grin. "I can't wait!"

Santa beamed. Rudolph might have had an odd looking nose, but he sure was a friendly one.

"We'll see you over at the workshop in a few minutes!" said Norman.

"Righty, ho!" said Santa.

 He then made his way over to the workshop. When he entered, he stood and laughed out loud. Thousands of elves broke into song when Santa stepped in.

"We wish you a Merry Christmas, We wish you a Merry Christmas

We wish you a Merry Christmas, and a Happy New Year!"

Santa joined in the singing and the workshop was filled with thousands of voices as they sang the song. When the song was finished, everyone let out whoops and cheers.

Santa's face glowed with happiness. His heart swelled as he looked at the thousands of elves, who were all smiling ear to ear.

"Ho! Ho! Ho!" boomed Santa. "And a Merry Christmas to each and every one of you!"

Amidst cheering, Santa walked to the back of the enormous workshop. The sleigh was already there and the reindeer were snorting and pawing at the ground. They were in pairs, except for Rudolph, who was by himself at the front. His nose was a bright, red light bulb, giving off a warm glow.

The sleigh was loaded up high with enormous sacks of presents. Everyone crowded around as Santa stepped up into the sleigh. Once settled on the seat, he pulled a thick quilt over his lap.

"You all did it!" said Santa. "You all got the gifts wrapped in time!"

"I told you we would," said Fergus. "We just couldn't let down all those boys and girls all over the world!"

The sleigh then moved slowly forward. Thousands of elves were gathered around and they shouted out, "Hip hip, hooray! Hip hip, hooray! Hip hip, hooray!"

Santa then shouted out, "Now Dasher, now Dancer, now Prancer, now Vixen. On Comet, on Cupid, on Donner, on Blitzen!" And then he gave one last shout, "On Rudolph!"

With that, as cheers rang in the air, the sleigh picked up speed. It went faster and faster and faster. Finally, to a giant cheer, it lifted up into the air.

The elves continued cheering as Santa and his sleigh climbed higher and higher into the velvet black night with the brightly shining stars.

"Look at Rudolph's nose!" said Norman. "It's shining so brightly you can see it from here!"

And it was true. Rudolph's nose, even from a distance, shone a bright red in the midnight sky. The elves continued to watch as Santa and his sleigh, small specks in the sky, passed through the full moon. It was a fantastic sight, and when they passed, the elves all gave each other a high five.

Christmas had been saved!

Epilouge

It was a week after Christmas and Santa and Mrs Claus were resting by the fireplace. Mrs Claus was knitting a sweater and Santa was enjoying a cup of hot chocolate.

"It was incredible!" said Santa. "We left presents under so many Christmas trees! And so many kids wrote us letters and left us treats. They left cookies for me and carrots for the reindeer!"

"And did you eat all the cookies?" asked Mrs Claus.

"Of course, I did!" said Santa, patting his big belly. "And you know what, Mrs Claus? I've realized something."

"What's that, Santy?" asked Mrs Claus, peering over her glasses at Santa.

"Well, do you remember that day when I found out about the reindeer and how the elves were slacking off?"

"Oh yes, Santy!" said Mrs Claus. "I was so worried!"

"I really thought Christmas was going to be ruined," said Santa. "I really did. But you know what? It's turned out to be the best Christmas ever!"

Mrs Claus smiled at Santa and patted his knee. "What do you mean by that?" she asked.

"Well, Comet is a fantastic reindeer. He's so fast, it's incredible! And Rudolph! That bright red, glowing nose of his came in so handy! It was like a guiding light! And he's such a lovely fellow!"

"That's fantastic, Santy!" said Mrs Claus.

"And those elves!" said Santa. "I was so upset with them! But they did the right thing in the end. They turned it around and worked their socks off. They proved to me that they were genuinely sorry. And I know that they'll never do it again!"

"I'm so happy to hear that!" said Mrs Claus. "I was surprised that you had quit that day. I knew that you must have been so upset to do that."

"Oh, I wouldn't really have quit," said Santa. "I was just so annoyed and upset at that moment. But no, I wouldn't have given up that easy. I would have tried my hardest for all the boys and girls around the world."

"Now, that's the Santy I know!" said Mrs Claus. They both settled back into their comfy chairs in front of the fireplace. Another year was over. Another year of bringing smiles to children all over the world.

So when it gets close to Christmas, you just never know. If you look closely into the dark, twinkling sky, you just might see Santa and his reindeer dashing by. And if you listen very closely, you just might hear, "HO, HO HO! MERRY CHRISTMAS!"

If you enjoyed reading this story, you may enjoy other books by Kate Clary! Please consider leaving a review on Amazon if you enjoyed this book!